WIFE TO BE

A Survivor's Guide

For the New & Not-So Newlywed

SAKINAH BUNCH

A Survivor's Guide

WIFE TO BE

To my husband for making this book possible and creating a safe haven for us to grow. I love you deeply.

To my mother and my nana, two strong women who poured their lives and love into me until the very end.

To my daughter, Divyne, and sons, Jonathan and Elijah, for being the eyes that watch me. May you, Divyne, become a Proverbs 31 woman and may you, my sons, marry women of this caliber.

To the many women throughout the years who have walked with me, prayed for me and blessed me in immeasurable ways, I cannot thank you enough. A special honorable mention goes to my Aunt Libby who continues to keep me on the straight and narrow and my photographer Sheryl Redmon, who has a way of capturing the true essence of people. Omar and I are grateful for your generosity and willingness to share your gift with us.

To the special woman who was responsible for the many nuggets of wisdom laced within these pages. You are joyfully referenced in this book as the "Wise Woman". You were insightful beyond your years. Your wisdom runs deep within my veins and permeates my spirit. I carry your words with me always. I am eternally grateful to you for caring enough about the sanctity of marriage and my husband and me to take me under your wing, mentor me and pray for me.

Most importantly, to all of the women who will read this book. May you be as blessed reading it as I was writing it. May your marriages be full of joy and may you all abound in wisdom. This book is dedicated to you.

A Survivor's Guide

God brought this beautiful woman into my life back in 1994 by way of a part-time telemarketing job where we both worked. We began seeing each other sometime after our initial meeting and dated for approximately three years prior to getting married and joining the United States Army. I could never have imagined then the woman and cook that she would blossom into! In fact, I remember the very first meal that she prepared for me like it was yesterday. She made barbecue chicken with something else that I cannot recall at this time. The chicken was truly unforgettable. I can vividly see myself sticking my fork and knife into it and the chicken yelling at me to stop hurting it! Yes, it was that horrible and raw! We made a collective decision to go out to eat that night.

Sakinah has always had a tremendous spirit and love for others. That spirit and love for others is what won me over (after her beauty). In the years since our initial "chicken dinner" her love for preparing food and seeing others enjoy her cooking has bloomed in a magnificent manner. I am truly amazed at how God (not sure why because He is all-powerful) used what could have been major setbacks in our life and turned it into a passion of hers...and made her good at it! When we found out about our daughter's severe food allergies, she could have just packed it in and followed the advice of traditional medical providers. She made it a point to get educated about the food allergies and sensitivities in order to get her baby healthy again! When we found out that I was diagnosed with a deficiency that significantly limits the types of foods I can eat, she did not flinch. She educated herself about the condition and now watches my food intake like a hawk! She truly found the balance between what is healthy and what tastes good.

Just about everyone who comes to our house for a meal gets the opportunity to have a home-cooked, healthy meal that is also delightful, delectable and delicious. All of her meals are also prepared with large amounts of love because she truly cares about what others put into their bodies. I am thrilled to see how many women this book will bless. Ladies, don't be afraid to share some of this with your husband or fiancée as the nuggets of knowledge she shares can benefit both of you. It is a true statement that "intimacy begins in the kitchen". Enjoy the reading because it will make a meaningful impact in your relationship with your significant other. I know this because the lessons she shares in this book come from our experiences together over the last two and half decades. I can tell you first-hand that it has been an incredible journey and I am extremely proud to be her co-pilot.

Omar Bunch

Husband, Father, U.S. Army Soldier

WIFE TO BE

Introduction

Picture it, you are snuggled in your favorite chair with your most treasured blanket. A double serving of your favorite piping hot beverage is sitting on the coffee table. You and your best friend are talking and having some much-needed girl time. No guys. No distractions. Just real heartfelt conversation. That is the essence of this book. No pretenses. No sugar-coated words. It is just the simple transparency of two close friends sharing life together.

We only have one rule here. Enjoy the fellowship. Every relationship is different in the nuances it produces. However, the overarching principles in this book are tried and true.

Each chapter has a story, reflection, real life application and recipe section. Some recipes will have a V, GF or P marked next to their title. This indicates whether the recipe is suitable or adaptive for a vegan, gluten-free and/or paleo eating style. Where you see an * in the vitamin/mineral section and you see it again next to a food item, it means that in order to have that vitamin or mineral present you must use that food item out of the options given. When a recipe calls for a sauce or stock, a gluten-free, vegan or paleo option is always inferred. All recipes serve four unless otherwise noted. The fresher the ingredients the better the recipes will turn out. Unlike many cookbooks you may be used to, the instructions in this book are meant to be added to the greatest and most important ingredient you will ever incorporate, which is *love*. So, feel free to have fun with the recipes. Add a little more here, take away something over there, make these your own. The goal is to get you used to feeling comfortable in the kitchen and helping you to realize that cooking is not about a regimental process. It is about adding heart and soul to your home and nourishment to your family and your life. Use this as your very own cookbook/workbook/life guide/journal. Feel free to write in it. Annotate your notes in the reflection and real-life application sections. Use this book as your personal journal. You will write all of your answers and results here. You will date when you begin an action and when you complete it. If there is anything abnormal or praiseworthy you will mark that in here too. When I first began to journal, about 5 years into my marriage, it was a release. I released anger, joy, sadness, gladness, disappointment, and accomplishments all onto its pages. It was my weight bearer. I have overflowed several journals since that first one. There is a joyful nostalgia that overcomes me when I look back over them to see how our marriage has grown. It is unbelievable and overwhelming. My hope is that you too will get much use out of your journal and keep it for years to come. So that one day a few decades from now, as you thumb through this book and your accompanying journal, you too will look back with fondness of the past and encouragement for the future.

A Survivor's Guide

Table of Contents

SURVIVAL TIP #1
PREP FOR THE MARRIAGE— NOT JUST THE WEDDING - **3**

SURVIVAL TIP #2
THE PRESSURE COOKER IS A NECESSITY - **14**

SURVIVAL TIP #3
MICROWAVE MARRIAGES DON'T LAST - **24**

SURVIVAL TIP #4
OVEN-BAKED DELIGHTS NOURISH THE UNION - **30**

SURVIVAL TIP #5
SOMETIMES MARRIAGE OFFERS SINGLE SERVINGS - **41**

SURVIVAL TIP #6
ALWAYS HAVE CHOCOLATE ON HAND - **53**

SURVIVAL TIP #7
I THINK I MAY NEED A DRINK: A MAN'S DEEPEST NEED - **62**

SURVIVAL TIP #8
A SUPPLEMENTAL PILL JUST WON'T DO - **72**

SURVIVAL TIP #9
EAT YOUR VEGGIES TO BE STRONG - **83**

SURVIVAL TIP #10
OLD-SCHOOL HOME COOKING: FIND A MENTOR AND A MENTEE - **92**

SURVIVAL TIP #11
DEVELOP THE NECK BONE: THE MAN IS THE HEAD BUT THE WOMAN IS THE NECK - **103**

SURVIVAL TIP #12
APHRODISIACS-R-US: THE SEX FACTOR – **113**

WIFE TO BE

A Survivor's Guide

Survival Tip #1

Prep for the Marriage— Not Just the Wedding

In 1997, I was living in Baltimore and was working as a secretary and data entry clerk. The agency I worked for was run by two successful women. One was the financial backer of the business, the other the mastermind. Neither was flashy or drove a fancy car, but their shoes were always on point. The duo unfailingly wore the latest Donna Karans, Stuart Weitzmans, or Salvatorre Ferragamos of the day. These ladies oozed girl power. I was inspired by their very presence, and I thoroughly enjoyed my job. Being there made me feel like I could run with the big dogs.

I was engaged to my then-fiancé, Omar. We were so excited to be getting married in two months. He had just finished his Army basic training in South Carolina and was about to be stationed in Ft. Bragg, North Carolina, so I told him I would take care of all of the wedding planning.

When my bosses found out I was getting married, one offered to host the wedding at her mansion. The three of us sat in the office and fantasized about the big day. Should it be held inside her gazillion square foot home? Ok, maybe it wasn't quite a gazillion square feet, but it was ginormous. We imagined how the train of my gown would look as I walked down the long, winding stairs into her oversized family room. How about a garden wedding beside the pool? I was on cloud nine. With the wedding venue set, my other boss offered to help with the catering. All Omar and I had to do was invite our families and it would be perfect.

As the big day grew closer, the anticipation built. One day, about two weeks before we got married, Omar called me at work. We'd gotten used to daydreaming about our future and talking about the wedding. However, this particular conversation was different. He was talking about some really deep stuff like moving to North Carolina and me being a military wife.

A military wife? It had never dawned on me that I would have to leave my life in Maryland and move to a completely new place. In my naive, 21-year-old mind, I thought Omar would do his soldier thing, and in a year or two, we would be back together.

I told Omar I had no plans to leave Baltimore. My family lived there. I had a job I enjoyed. My apartment was comfortable. Why would I want to leave all of that?

The phone line went silent. I had to say hello three times to make sure he was still there. I heard him sigh heavily in disappointment and disbelief. When he finally gathered his thoughts, he exclaimed, "Are you serious? We are getting married. Why wouldn't we live together?"

The answer flew out of my mouth.

"Because I am not going to follow you all around the world like some puppy dog," I snapped. "I love you, but I am not going to give up everything in my life for you every time the Army tells you that you have to move!"

Wow! When I heard the cutting words that flew from my own lips, I knew I'd hurt him. Anger, pity, and frustration filled me. How could he just assume? He knew me! In my mind, he should have known that it was completely out of my character to follow a man around. Looking back, I wonder how we got far enough to plan on getting married yet never talked about the day after our wedding, the week after, or the lifetime after. We had been together for three years. Neither of us considered what we were really getting ourselves into.

Both of us feeling slighted, we said goodbye and hung up. There were only two weeks until we said, "I do." We each had to collect whatever hopes we had of happily ever after and either throw them in the trash or revise the plan.

Magic Has a Cost

If you're anything like I was, the idea of getting married is magical. You imagine yourself looking absolutely beautiful! You dream about the flowing train of your gown, held up by six ladies-in-waiting as you walk down the aisle. You picture the yellow and white tulip centerpieces on each table, the hors-d'oeuvres, the perfect cake. This day is all about you, right? Or is it?

Billions of dollars are spent each year on weddings in the United States. Couples spent an average of $33,391 on weddings in 2017, according to a study conducted by The Knot: (https://bit.ly/2FycQmH). Many take over a year to plan their big day.

Yet how much of that money and time is invested in marital counseling, financial planning, and simply talking about the future? Like Omar and I, many couples tend to spend much more time preparing for the wedding than for the marriage. Unless you're an average Hollywood celebrity, your marriage will far outlast the day you say "I do."

WIFE TO BE

It's easy to fall in love with the idea of getting married. But it's smart to prepare for and fully embrace the reality of *being* married.

What excites you more — your wedding day, or the days, months, and years after? Have you and your spouse-to-be talked about where you'll live? How many children, if any, will you have, and how will they be raised? What are your religious affiliations? Where will you spend major holidays? On the following page is a list of conversation starters you and your future spouse can use. Although not exhaustive, these questions are a great way to begin thinking about your life after the big day.

A Survivor's Guide

Survival Tip #1 – Reflection Questions

1. What is communication like in your family? How do you resolve arguments?

    The answer to these questions will give you great insight into his psyche and how he may choose to resolve arguments with you in the future. If he's used to dealing with disagreements by leaving, that red flag should be addressed before you exchange your vows. This can indicate a pattern of failure to follow through on commitments or a breakdown in communication later on.

2. What do you love about me? Which of my characteristics do you find irritating? What would you like me to change?

    Listen carefully here to his answer. What he may find cute or even slightly annoying now can turn into a raging river of division in a year or two. Knowing this up front will help the two of you and hopefully deflect arguments that begin with the words "Well, you knew this about me before we got married..."

3. How much time should we spend with each other's families? How often should our families visit us? How and where do you see us spending important holidays?

    These are important questions! My husband and I fought on many occasions; Thanksgiving, Christmas, and especially Mother's Day, because we each wanted to visit our families who lived in two separate states. Discussing these things will not only reveal whether you have a momma's boy who is a Ray Barone, but also help you establish healthy boundaries for each family's involvement in your home and relationship.

4. Do you see us having children? If so, when, and how many do you envision?

    My husband is one of six children and each of his parents came from families considerably larger than that! I assumed he wanted a houseful of kids, too. Imagine my surprise after our wedding day when he said he didn't want any! Although his stance changed and we now have three beautiful children, this doesn't always happen. Don't dismiss his answer to this question, and don't think you'll sway him into wanting what you want. Address the topic of children before the marriage so you can understand each other's feelings and prevent future disagreements.

5. What is your credit score and level of debt?

Many newly married couples don't realize that when they say "I do," they're also saying, "I do" to each other's debt. This question is a key indicator of his relationship with money. Is he a spendthrift? Does money run through his hands like water? Is it more important for him to drive a brand-new car rather than move out of his mother's basement? (By the way, if the answer to the last question is yes, RUN, GIRL, RUN and don't look back!

6. Where do you see us in five years, ten years, and twenty years?

Time lapses are important. It gives you a sneak peek into his hopes and dreams for the two of you. It allows you to understand where his thought pattern is with his life and whether he sees you two elevating your lives, remaining stagnant or moving backward. A man with a vision is truly one to be cherished.

7. What or who is the foundation of your spiritual life?

This is so important. The Bible tells us that we are not to be unequally yoked. No matter your spiritual affiliation, there are some real truths here. It is difficult to be yoked with someone and walk in opposite directions. In the best-case scenario, you'll end up with severe lacerations. In the worst case, you'll choke to death and die. The same picture can be painted in a relationship. If two people are walking in two totally different directions, the relationship will suffer. Make sure the two of you are in agreement in this area.

∞ ∞ ∞

Real Life Application – Journal Entry #1

How have you prepared for your wedding day? Have you spent as much time preparing for the days, months, and years after? Make a list of things you have done to prepare for your wedding day that will also benefit your married life. What are some things you think you may need to add to that list to make your marriage prep just as phenomenal as your wedding day?

A Survivor's Guide

Survival Tip #1 Notes

WIFE TO BE

Survival Tip #1 Notes

Easy Meal Prep Recipes

Preparing meals in advance saves time and money.

Pulled Jackfruit (V, GF, P) - *Vitamin C, magnesium, potassium*

Ingredients:
- 2 cloves Garlic finely chopped
- 1/2 sweet onion sliced
- 2 20 oz cans Young green jackfruit
- 1 can or 1 whole fresh pineapple diced,
- ½ tsp black pepper
- 3 sweet peppers (small)
- ¾ - 1 cup of your favorite BBQ sauce
- 1 tbsp avocado or coconut oil
- 1/4 cup vegetable broth or water

Directions:

1. Sauté onions in a skillet with coconut oil.
2. Pour jackfruit in crockpot making sure to separate. If too tough skip this step until almost done.
3. Simmer all ingredients in a crockpot on low for 6 hours or until pull apart soft and tender.
4. Divide and put jackfruit into 4 separate containers.
5. Great served over quinoa, rice, or pasta. Tasty as an hors d'oeuvre served over crackers or toast.

Banana Mango "Ice Cream" *(No ice cream maker needed)*

(V, GF, P) – *Vitamins B6 & C, manganese, potassium*

Ingredients: (Serves 4-6 individual servings**):**

- 8 frozen large bananas thickly sliced (it is best to slice bananas and put into a freezer bag before placing them in the freezer)
- 1 cup coconut "cream" (use cream from canned coconut milk, but **do not** add the milk portion)
- 1 cup frozen mangoes diced
- ¼ cup cranberries
- 1 tsp vanilla (optional)
- 2 tsp coconut sugar or maple syrup (optional)
- Add any of your favorite toppings. In my house we love GF homemade granola

Directions:

1. Add bananas and coconut cream to blender a little at a time.
2. Once bananas and cream are slightly blended, (don't allow it to become liquidy) add mangoes and blend to desired consistency.
3. Pour into airtight freezer safe container. We like to have individual containers. Great for meal prep or when we are feeling territorial with our food.

Survival Tip #2

The Pressure Cooker is a Necessity

The Gentrys, a well-seasoned couple in their 60s, had the perfect marriage. Mr. Gentry was debonair, a man's man and definitely not hard on the eyes. Mrs. Gentry typified a lady in every sense of the word. She was gentle, delicate, and beauty personified. Honestly, I believe the woman could have walked on water. She was so regal. The Gentrys were always pleasant to each other, tender, and devoted.

Omar and I looked up to this couple. As our wedding day approached, I remember thinking in my heart, "I hope my marriage will mirror theirs." But secretly in my head I was thinking, "If this lasts five years or more, we'll be doing great."

Six months after Omar and I married, I could feel the storm brewing. We fought like heavyweight contenders with our words. Restraint was not in our vocabulary. The goal was to tear each other down with the harshest words possible. We threw the D-word — divorce — around like a baseball. It's funny how bona fide bliss can quickly turn to mastered misery. We went through trials that even some of the strongest marriages we knew did not endure.

We waged war for about two years. No couple can live like this for long and claim to have a healthy marriage. Emotional divorce is just as bad as physical divorce, in my opinion.

It gets tiring fighting like cats and dogs day after day, month after month, year after year. It got to the point that we could look into each other's eyes and see that we didn't have much more fight left in us. We were weary and worn. Therefore, we came to a meeting of the minds. First, we agreed to create a safe haven for us either to connect, or at least, not kill each other. That began with throwing the D-word out of our vocabularies. This kept us from seeing each other as enemy number one and opened up the opportunity for dialogue. With the bullseye no longer on each other's backs, healing could begin.

I recall a time when he came home from work. I was in the room rocking our daughter, who had been up all night, to sleep. She must have been about two or three months at this point. Each morning he would do physical training (exercise) with his unit. He would then come home, shower, change, sometimes grab a quick bite to eat and head out the door to work, most mornings without a word. This morning however, was abnormal. I heard the key go into the door lock. Although exhausted, I was readying myself for the fight. I thought if this man comes in and wakes this girl up, it is going to be on! When he came in, instead of making all sorts of noise as usual, he entered the house as quiet as a mouse. He shut the door quietly. I could hear faint steps walking toward the room. He peeped his head in and gestured to show me the bag of food he picked up just for me. I was floored. For the first time in a while I was able to slightly put my guard down. For the first time in years, I saw the man that I had married. There was still a hint of compassion left in him. There was still hope.

Pressure Cooker 101 - The Fundamentals

The pressure cooker is one of life's modern marvels. It can take a frozen roast and make it a savory soup in about an hour. Not in the mood for soup? Looking for a treat to satisfy your sweet tooth? You can also use a pressure cooker to create a delicious, decadent cheesecake or apple crisp in about 40 minutes. Pretty much anything you can cook on the stove or in the oven, you can make in a pressure cooker.

The technology behind this contemporary phenomenon is nothing short of amazing. Created in the 1600's, it uses advancements that were ahead of its time. Steam pressure is used to cook the food rapidly while maintaining the nutrients and magnifying the flavor of the dish. This works because the steam pressure builds inside of a sealed pot. The pressure mounts and brings the boiling point of water higher than the normal two hundred twelve degrees Fahrenheit it normally takes for water to boil. Because of this, instead of the contents becoming rubbery sitting in liquid, they become more moist, flavorful and desirable. In modern day pressure cookers there is a safety valve that does not permit the pot to be opened while the contents are under pressure. This limits burns, kitchen mishaps and full on explosions. The pressure cooker does to food what trials and tribulations should do to marriages.

Sometimes we look at a couple with a great marriage and believe the relationship was an overnight success. What we don't see is all the stress that produced those results. That couple may have dealt with miscommunication, lack of communication, loneliness, infidelity, lack of intimacy, feelings of insecurity, debt, emotional divorce and other trials. We don't know the necessary pressure that needed to be applied to create that successful marriage. The saying, "Never compare someone's outside to your inside" holds true.

Wisdom has shown me the Gentry's marriage took time and even pressure to cultivate. I never knew any of the struggles they went through. I suppose it was not my place to know. Perhaps their covenant with each other was to keep house business just that: house business. Their example has made me appreciate the pressure-cooker moments in my own marriage. The worst time ever in our marriage were the days we lived in North Carolina. They were dark. They were depressing. They were downright miserable. We fought constantly and I suppose since neither of us had our immediate family close, we felt isolated and alone. I wouldn't wish those days on anyone. Yet, because of those days we were knit together closer than we ever knew we could be. In those days, I couldn't see us lasting another year. Now two decades later we look back on those days and are grateful. Those may have been Gentry moments. Who knows? However, our marriage has benefited from those pressure cooker moments and has afforded us the opportunity to know each other and grow with each other strengthening our union each and every day.

Survival Tip #2 - Reflection Questions

1. Who is that "perfect" couple for you? How do they epitomize a healthy marriage?

2. Don't know that "perfect" pair? Envision a couple in your mind. What characteristics do you think they should have?

Real Life Application - Journal Entry #2

1. If you have identified that couple, ask them to share some of their pressure-cooker moments with you. Their wisdom may prove to be invaluable later on for you and your spouse.

2. If you have not identified that one them as of yet, find couples that display characteristics you would like to mirror in your marriage. If that is not possible, perhaps you can seek out another woman to talk with, who is successful in areas you would like to improve.

A Survivor's Guide

Survival Tip #2 Notes

Survival Tip #2 Notes

Pressure Cooker Recipes

Mushroom, Spinach, and Coconut Soup (V, GF, P)

- B vitamins, vitamins A, D* & K, copper, antioxidants

Ingredients:

- 2 cans coconut milk
- 1 ½ cups veggie stock
- 4-5 handfuls spinach
- 5-7 button or 4 shitake* mushrooms, sliced
- tbsp coconut sugar
- ½ tsp smoked paprika
- ¼ tsp turmeric
- ¼ tsp black pepper
- ¾ tsp sea salt
- 2 tsp curry
- Optional: 1 lb. of chicken or turkey breast, sliced (omit for vegan option)

Directions:

1. Put coconut milk (cream included) and veggie broth into Instant Pot/pressure cooker. Stir until combined.
2. Put the rest of the ingredients into Instant Pot/pressure cooker. Stir until spinach and mushrooms are coated with coconut/veggie mixture.
3. Set Instant Pot/pressure cooker to the "Soup" setting (18 minutes to pressurize).
4. Quick release the pressure or let simmer. Serve with toasted garlic bread or brown rice. The flavors blend

WIFE TO BE

Chicken or Mushroom Stew (V, GF, P)

- Antioxidants, vitamin K, fiber

Ingredients:

- 8 cups veggie broth
- 4 sweet peppers
- 2 celery stalks
- 1 medium onion
- 2 cloves garlic or any other fun combo of herbs, veggies, and spices that you desire (remember food is fun)
- 2 lbs. chicken legs (or 1 lb. portabella mushrooms sliced for a plant-based option)

Directions:

1. Place 8 cups of veggie broth and all ingredients into Instant Pot/pressure cooker.
2. Put the Instant Pot/pressure cooker on the "Chicken" setting for 18 minutes.
3. Voila, it is done!
4. Pairs well with some quinoa and a salad.

Survival Tip #3

Microwave Marriages Don't Last

Before marriage was even a thought in either of our minds, Omar and I dated. Well, if you define dating as meeting and a couple of months later shacking up, then yes, that is what we did. Our relationship went from zero to sixty in less than six seconds. There was no doubt about it; we were both physically attracted to one another. His smile and eyes hooked me the moment I saw him. My charm and smile won him over. Yup, we were hot and "in love." We were a match made in heaven. I knew his favorite number. He knew my favorite color. Our eyes couldn't meet without a twinkle appearing. We were so deep. We were marriage material for sure (insert eye roll here).

In reality, we were the prime example of a microwave relationship. The antithesis of a pressure cooker is a microwave. Sure, both cook foods more quickly than the conventional oven and the slow cooker, but the technology behind each is drastically different.

The pressure cooker applies intense amounts of physical force on the ingredients inside in order to cook them to perfection. The microwave, on the other hand, uses heat energy to quickly cook foods from the outside in. This process is very similar to how the sun bakes our skin when we're exposed to it. If we're not protected from the sun's rays, we end up severely burned.

The whole purpose of a microwave is to quickly heat food. If the food is left in the microwave too long or uncovered, it explodes and makes a mess all over the place. The food also rapidly cools down. Microwave marriages are very similar. Marriages that have neither firm foundation nor depth of relationship tend to quickly heat up, become volatile, then quickly cool down. There is not enough time to cultivate and mature a relationship between two people. In microwave marriages, the exterior of each person is the main focus. Not much focus is given to the interior part, the relational facet. You know, the aspect of marriage that comes into play when the money is not right, the sex is not as good as it used to be and looks fade. The real part of marriage is where the exteriors are shed and the interior is all you have left. Microwave relationships, left in that state, have a fast start, but a furious end.

Survival Tip #3 - Reflection Questions

1. How did your relationship begin?

2. After reading this chapter, would you describe your relationship as one built on love or lust?

3. What would you say is the foundation that upholds your union? Is that foundation firm or weak? One way to know is to evaluate your discussions. Do you two have any deep meaningful dialogue, or are your conversations mainly superficial?

∞ ∞ ∞

Real Life Application – Journal Entry #3

Building upon question #3 in Survival Tip #3, take a moment to reflect on how you two met and the progression of your relationship from then until now. Would you classify your relationship as one built on a firm foundation or more microwaved in nature? If it is a firm foundation, list 3-5 aspects that make that foundation strong. If you believe it is more microwave in nature, what steps can you take to strengthen it?

A Survivor's Guide

Survival Tip #3 Notes

WIFE TO BE

Survival Tip #3 Notes

A Survivor's Guide

Microwave Recipes

There are none! Did we not just talk about how microwave marriages don't last? We are working on marriages that are in it for the long haul in this book. I will forgive you this time for looking for recipes here but trust me you don't want that kind of recipe. No worries. Let's just move on to the next chapter No nutritional facts here either!

WIFE TO BE

Survival Tip #4

Oven-Baked Delights Nourish the Union

My momma said, "Do not trust another woman with your man!" What she meant by this was do not share information about your relationship, have your husband help in any way with (solo), or leave him open and vulnerable to another woman. It doesn't matter whether she is your best friend, acquaintance, or teller at the bank. She said you can be cordial, but the details about your relationship always remain just between you and your husband. She painted this vivid picture for me of how I would give another woman all of the tools she needed to position herself in just the right spot to be his comforter in the event he would need one. And according to her, there would *always* be an event when he would need a comforter and she would know exactly how to swoop in and help.

Although she was not always the best relationship expert on what to do, she did know exactly what *not* to do! I followed that type of advice because her words held truth. I invariably followed her *what not to do* advice because she gave it referencing potential marital affairs. On this particular day, that I will share, I was blindsided. I learned a whole new level of the saying never trust a woman with your man. Since I didn't see this scenario coming, I am going to give you this one piece of advice that if you heed it, will serve you well for many decades to come. Unless your man is physically abusive to you, be very careful even when talking with family about your relationship. (And for goodness sake, please do not bash your husband to other people.) Even if you share your relationship troubles with only family, they tend to have long memories and will recall all of the negative things your husband has done at the most inopportune times. You and your husband will have since made up, but the family will still brood over what you said he did last week. They hold on to it. Even when all is well, the next time he does something even slightly off in their opinion, your family will remind you what he did the last time. Your wounds will reopen about this event, that event, and perhaps future events. Your emotional wounds will grow deeper, making reconciliation all the more difficult.

I made this mistake before. During the first year of my marriage, I was livid with my husband. I don't even recall about what, I just remember that I could feel heat around my neck I was so angry. He seemed flippant and careless about whatever it was we were arguing about. I made the mistake of telling my mother (who, might I remind you, was not the best relationship expert).

I believe her exact words were, "I told you — you shouldn't have married him. Now, look at the mess you're in."

My mother began to berate my husband, calling him every name other than a child of God (which at the time he was not, but neither was I). At that moment, I heard my words coming out of her mouth. She was spewing back to me all of the malicious things I said about him in the past. I was not only furious with him, but also fuming at her. She was my mom and was supposed to encourage me, not tear down my choices. I was infuriated with myself because I had shared way too much information with her.

I was also dumbfounded at how I got myself into this predicament in the first place. I left my mother's house that day feeling deeply wounded and depleted. I felt like I was in a boxing match and my opponents were the very people I thought were in my corner. I felt like screaming, "Calgon take me away!" I wanted to escape. I not only wanted to leave my husband, but also wanted to leave everyone involved.

That sounds drastic, I am well aware. But the examples of marriage I saw as a child shifted into two extremes. On one hand, marriage was nothing more than a contract that could easily be broken. The possibility of divorce was always on the table and in many cases never the last resort. On the other hand, couples stayed together, but were emotionally divorced. They, more often than not, stayed together for a plethora of societal reasons: to save face, for the kids, financial implications and so on. So, at this stage of my marriage, I thought I had only two choices: either stay in this marriage and be miserable or get a divorce.

Thankfully, there was a third choice. From that day forward, I made up my mind that I didn't want to have a marriage like the ones I witnessed growing up. I did not want to have an ex-husband or baby-daddy. I wanted my marriage to work. I decided that certain adjustments needed to be made and the first adjustment was me. I made a vow to my husband that what happened in our house stayed in our house. Nothing would be revealed without the permission of the other person involved. This still holds true today. Keeping the relational oven closed creates the safe haven that your marriage needs and builds the boundaries that establish love and respect.

Meat that is baked in an oven should stay in there until done. The cardinal rule in cooking is to open the oven only when absolutely necessary. By doing so, you allow the meat to cook evenly and the end result is more tender and juicy. When you open the oven door, you run the risk of letting out the heat and making the cook time longer. Meat that's not heated evenly isn't as tender, tasty, or tantalizing.

What holds true for the food of your body also holds true for the nourishment of your relationship. What goes on between you and the person you have chosen to spend the rest of your life with should stay with the two of you. Do not open your relationship oven to others. Give your marriage the opportunity to become tender, ready to withstand the blades of life that will attack. This is part of creating that safe haven we talked about in Survival Tip #2, the Pressure Cooker chapter.

Trust me, everyone will have an opinion about your relationship, about what you should do and where he should go. Remember that it is you who said "I do." You and your family did not say "I do." You did. There is a tradition of giving the bride away. It is still implemented today. The Bible, in agreement, says there is a leaving and cleaving that takes place and unites your two souls together. You have now left your family to be united with this one person for life. So, let's talk about how you two can mesh and create this one body union.

Survival Tip #4 - Reflection Questions

1. What safeguards have you and your spouse implemented to make sure that your oven stays closed and only opened when the circumstance necessitates?

2. If you haven't given this area much thought, what do you think would be the first step you both should take in order to begin the dialog for creating this safe haven?

∞ ∞ ∞

Real Life Application – Journal Entry #4

1. Was there a time when you opened your relational oven and it hurt your spouse? If so, go to him and ask his forgiveness. Start the process of creating a safe haven by asking his forgiveness in the area and making a verbal pact to keep house business (relationship business) just between the two of you? Has your spouse done this to you? Forgive him. He does not need to know that you are forgiving him for the occurrence just do it and move on.

2. If you have never had a conversation with your spouse about safeguarding your relational oven, now is the time. Compare your answers from the reflection section with his answers to see if you both agree on what a safe haven looks like.

3. Create a written covenant between the two of you that you both will sign. This covenant is to show the seriousness and commitment the two of you have in this area for one another. Have it signed by a trusted friend/couple as a witness(es) who will also keep you accountable.

A Survivor's Guide

Survival Tip #4 Notes

Survival Tip #4 Notes

A Survivor's Guide

Oven-Baked Recipes

BBQ Cauliflower Bites (V, GF, P) - *Folate, vitamin C & K, fiber*

Ingredients:

- 1 cauliflower head
- Your favorite BBQ sauce
- 2 cups quinoa flour or rice flour
- Seasonings of choice (I love to use curry, smoked paprika, black pepper and garlic)

Directions:

1. Heat oven to 450°F.
2. Break cauliflower into large florets.
3. Lightly steam cauliflower until it is slightly wet but remains firm. (This will help the flour to stick). You can also coat cauliflower with egg or maple syrup (vegan option).
4. Season quinoa flour or rice flour with your favorite seasonings.
5. Coat cauliflower with seasoned quinoa flour or rice flour.
6. Place cauliflower on parchment paper in a baking pan.
7. Bake at 450°F for 5 minutes.
8. Remove cauliflower from oven. Coat cauliflower with BBQ sauce and bake until the tips are crispy (about another 15-20 minutes).

WIFE TO BE

Coconut-Crusted Flounder (GF, P) - *Protein, selenium, fiber*

Ingredients:

- 4 flounder fillets
- ¾ tsp garlic
- ¼ tsp sea salt
- ¼ tsp black pepper
- ¼ tsp smoked paprika
- Fresh or dried dill to taste
- 1 egg or just wet the fish (to adhere breading)
- 1 cup shredded unsweetened coconut

Directions:

1. Preheat oven to 400°F
2. Mix shredded coconut and seasonings let sit for 5 minutes
3. Mix egg in a bowl
4. Place parchment paper in oven pan
5. Dip flounder into egg, then dip it into seasoned coconut breading
6. Place fish on parchment paper
7. Bake at 400°F for 15 min.

A Survivor's Guide

Survival Tip #5

Sometimes Marriage Offers Single Servings

Coming home to an empty house each night became my norm. I almost appreciated it, because it was better than being in the house with the wordless stranger. The person I said I would spend the rest of my life with no longer inhabited this house. We were growing farther and farther apart and I didn't know what to do to rekindle the flame that now didn't even resemble a spark. I got the "It's not you; it's me," routine. Oh man, that is *so* not comforting.

I suggested we go to marital counseling, something we probably should have done *before* we said our vows. I attended this little church, near where we lived of which both of us were a little skeptical. Omar had a disdain for this church more than I. He would not attend with me, but he was willing to attempt marital counseling sessions facilitated by the pastor.

I noticed our counseling sessions became more and more one-sided. As the pastor leaned back in his leather office chair, reclined and smug, he began bashing Omar about miniscule things. His main topic of discussion was my husband's sporadic church attendance. I tried to look straight ahead and not stare at either of them, but I was feeling uncomfortable enough for the both of us. I could sense Omar's temperature rising and nose flaring. I couldn't see how any good was going to come out of this. To put it mildly, these counseling sessions clearly were a bust. My husband and I both agreed that these sessions had to cease. Our plight almost seemed like a hopeless cause and our relationship became even more strained. It was, however, the first time we agreed on just about anything. And that was good because we later found out that the pastor used to be a pimp, and he had many children outside of the union of he and his wife. Not really someone's number one pick for a marriage counselor, which leads me back to Survival Tip #4: Be very careful who you talk to about your marriage and from whom you receive counsel.

So, if going to the church didn't solve our dilemma, what would? With counseling shot down, we were losing hope fast for our happily ever after. We not only felt hopeless, but helpless. Although my husband could feel the chasm ever widening between us, he didn't see how any of it was his doing. I will be the first to admit that it takes two to tango. We both had a hand in creating this mayhem. I cannot point the finger at him without at least three more fingers pointing back at me. I, too, played a significant role in how the relationship was deteriorating. I was that nagging wife to whom no man wants to be married. Using words to tear down your mate day after day does something to the psyche. The one great thing I got from those two marital counseling sessions was that if I desired for there to be change, that change needed to start with me. One of my husband's coworkers, we will refer to her here as the Wise Woman, poured so much of her wisdom into my life during this time. A time when I needed it most. Although she didn't know either of us very well, she saw through our facades. She didn't hesitate to share her insights with me, but she did so with such gentleness and love. "You cannot change him," I would hear her say. "The only person you can change is you. Therefore, continue to work on you and pray earnestly for him." Those words went straight through to my core. To have someone see me, see my struggle and not sugar coat what was going on and just be real with me without bashing him, was unreal to me. I cherished her honesty and humility. I cherished her!

I didn't want to end up like my mother, who for years was a single mom. Through the muffled tears on her pillow, I uncovered just a glimpse of how hard life was for her. I saw how she performed on a daily basis the tasks of both mother and father. No one should have to do that. That is a heavy burden of responsibility to shoulder. It is not fair to the children and it is not fair to the parent. I didn't want her story to be my story. I applaud her for being such a strong woman and instilling that strength and endurance in me. At the same time, if I could avoid ever having to know that life firsthand, or have my children hear my muted cries, I would do whatever it took, within Godly boundaries, to keep my marriage together. And if that meant working on me, even though at the time I didn't notice the depth of my issues, I was willing to do this.

Throughout this time, the Wise Woman shared verses with me that will never leave me as long as I live. "It is better to live in a corner of the roof than in a house shared with a contentious woman." (Proverbs 25:24 NASB). This opened my eyes to why he never wanted to be home when I was home. Moreover, by nagging, I was helping him choose to leave rather than stay and work it out. In the same regard, he helped me choose the various methods I did when he was nonchalant and acted as if he didn't care. We continued like this for 2 years.

Our turning point was when I fully embraced the following Bible verses:

"What therefore God has joined together let no man separate" (Mark 10:9 NKJV).

"Even if some do not obey the word, they without a word, may be won by the *conduct* of their wives" (1 Peter 3:1 NKJV).

In plain English, these verses mean because God brought us together, we should not allow anyone — not even ourselves — to divide us. The 1 Peter verse states that if my husband is not acting right, I must first look within to see if my behavior has something to do with it. Not to say the wife is to blame for the husband's behavior, but it should give us cause to look inward and check ourselves to make sure we are not in the wrong before we address our husbands' actions. Later on, in the chapter, it talks about having a gentle and quiet spirit. To me, that was even more foreign than just changing my nagging ways and behavior. I was so used to using my words to convey how I felt that I didn't realize the strength of nonverbal language. I misunderstood the power purposeful silence wielded to gain the attention of the person to whom it is aimed. Not in an "I'm not talking to you" manner, but a tool far greater and deeper than the conscience can fathom. The power of remaining silent when we could defend ourselves or lash out at our spouses displays tremendous strength. It not only stops many arguments as one cannot argue alone, but it gives God the time to work in our spouses lives, because our husbands' ears are no longer being crowded out by our voice. They are now able to hear God's still small voice. The voice that can move mountains.

These two Bible verses allowed me to see that if I wanted him to change his behavior, I needed to change mine. I couldn't expect him to be loving and caring when I was nagging and berating. It also shed light on the fact that it was hard for my husband to hear the voice of God when I was a clanging cymbal in his ear. It was time for me to move out of the way and let God work on him while I worked on me.

I heard it is said that being married cures loneliness. Let's go ahead and squash this myth right now. Being married will not solve a loneliness issue any more than being in a gym will solve a weight issue. In some cases, being married may intensify loneliness. Sometimes you can feel completely alone even though your husband is right there with you each day.

Before the wedding, most view marriage like the movie "Jerry Maguire." (If you haven't seen it please go stream it; it's full of gems.) This movie stars Tom Cruise as sports agent Jerry Maguire, and Renee Zellweger, who plays Jerry's wife, Dorothy. In the film's climactic scene, Jerry, who is separated from his wife, interrupts a women's meeting held at their home. He tells the women, "Hello," and that he is looking for his wife. When Dorothy appears, he begins to go through this whole monologue about how he was wrong and misses her and how they should be together. Then utters the words, "You...complete me," with a tear in his eye. Dorothy responds, "You had me at hello." They embrace and the world is wonderful again.

But that is Hollywood. What happens when your husband deviates from the script and that fairytale scene is not your reality? What happens when it feels like your best friend is a continent away, only to roll over and see he is lying less than 12 inches from you each and every night? How do you overcome this? Obviously, this was not what you envisioned when you looked into his winsome, dreamy eyes and pledged your undying commitment to him. How do you overcome the deafening silence of words unsaid? How do you keep it all together and not blow up or become like I was initially — the wife who nagged and wept all the time?

Hopefully the reflection questions on the next page will help you sort through the montage of feelings you may be going through. Loneliness may be the place you find yourself in either now or perhaps at some point during your marriage, but it doesn't have to be a life sentence. There is hope.

Survival Tip #5 - Reflection Questions

1. What are some myths you believed about marriage? Are you finding any to be true? Explain.

2. What is the best thing you can do to help alleviate or prevent loneliness in your marriage?

3. If you are in this predicament now, what do you believe are some root causes of your loneliness?

4. Do you believe your husband feels the same? Why or why not?

Real Life Application - Journal Entry #4

Look up the scripture Hebrews 11:1. Read it word for word slowly. Define hope. Define faith. How can you apply this scripture to your life not matter your circumstance? What do you think God is trying to tell you?

A Survivor's Guide

Survival Tip #5 Notes

Survival Tip #5 Notes

Loneliness Comfort Desserts

Apple Crisp Topped with Vanilla Banana Ice Cream

(V, GF, P) - *Fiber, potassium, vitamin C*

Ingredients: (serves 1... a couple of times over)

- 3 gala apples
- 4 Tbsp coconut sugar
- ¾ cup coconut oil
- ½ cup almonds
- ¼ teaspoon salt
- ½ teaspoon ground orange peel
- ¼ teaspoon vanilla

Directions:

1. Slice apples & chop almonds (set aside)
2. Melt coconut oil on medium heat in frying pan
3. Place apples in pan (should sizzle)
4. Add orange peel, salt, vanilla and sugar, then mix
5. Add almonds mix then lower heat to simmer
6. Let simmer until apples are soft

Vanilla Banana ice cream
Ingredients:

- 4 frozen bananas
- ¼ cup vanilla yogurt (milk or coconut based)
- ¼ cup almond milk

Directions:

1. Mix all ingredients in blender
2. Place atop of apple crisp, garnish with chopped almonds and bacon (plant-based bacon for vegan option) and serve.

Red, White and Cream Coconut Delight (V, GF, P)

– Antioxidants, vitamin C, fiber, manganese

Ingredients: (serves 1)

- 1 can coconut cream (refrigerated overnight unopened)
- ½ cup coconut flakes
- 2 pinches cinnamon
- ¼ cup mango chunks
- ¼ cup blueberries
- ¼ cup strawberries sliced
- ¼ cup cranberries
- ½ cup GF granola or chopped nuts

Directions:

1. Blend coconut cream, cinnamon, and mango chunks in a blender until fluffy. (A hand blender works best.)
2. Place alternating layers of nuts, fruit, and cream in a bowl until the bowl is full. Sprinkle coconut flakes on the top.
3. Enjoy!

A Survivor's Guide

Survival Tip #6

Always Have Chocolate on Hand

I have a couple of foods that I truly crave every once in a while. One of those is chocolate. And it cannot be just any chocolate, it must be a particular chocolate. My family knows I am not one who is big on receiving gifts. That is not the language of love for me, but if they do decide to love me through gift giving, they know I spell love H-E-R-S-H-E-Y-'-S N-U-G-G-E-T-S. Yes, Hershey's Nuggets are my vice. Not the kisses (that's not enough chocolate) and not the bar because it gives me a stomachache. It has to be the nuggets, because that is just the right amount to satisfy me.

We, as women, have an innate need to be loved. For us, love can be shown in a variety of ways. Love can be expressed through gifts, acts of service, words of affirmation and so on. But however you experience love, understand your spouse may not experience love as you do. In fact, the need for love may not even be as serious for him as it is for you. In the Bible, God commands husbands to love their wives. Why do you think God needed to command husbands to do this? I'm glad you asked that question. It is because in us, love is instinctive, but in men ... not so much. God knew how he formed men. He knew he'd have to command men to show love and outward affection (that doesn't necessarily lead to sex) for it to be at the forefront of their minds. So, you may be asking, if love is not men's top priority, then what is? Again, another great question which will be handled in a later chapter. This chapter is about love; this chapter is about you.

Why do you think God did not need to command women to love? We are loving beings by nature. We are nurturers. For quite a few of us, we have fallen in love with love. When love is around, everything is alright. Now please don't misunderstand me, men need love, too. It is just not as high on their radar as it is on ours.

Now that you are armed with this information, you can thank me, because it will prevent many fights (I like to call them moments of intense fellowship), when you may not feel that your spouse is loving you. It very well may be that he is giving you the thing he needs in the only way that he knows how. Again, we will address what he needs later.

It is our job as wives to help our husbands see how to love us. But first you must ask yourself this question, "Do *you* love you?" I mean, do you *really* love every aspect about yourself? This is an important question, because sometimes we are not looking for our spouse to love us, we are looking for our spouse to validate or complete us. That is not their job. I was listening to a motivational video by Will Smith yesterday. He was sharing how he asked his wife, Jada, what makes her happy. She said something to the effect that she is not responsible for his happiness and he is not responsible for hers. Oh, such truth. We women must first look into the mirror and be comfortable, content, and love — yes, love — the person staring back at us. If we don't everything our husbands say or do will be viewed through a tainted lens. Nothing he does will ever be satisfying, at least not long-term. The secret to having a happy marriage full of contentment and love is to first be comfortable with the main company you keep, and that is you.

Among my many wonderful talents, I had a knack of seeing all of the positive things in everyone else and all of the faults in me. From my personality, to intelligence, to my physical features there was a self-loathing that was present that clouded my vision. Finally, a friend of mine asked me point blank, why I hated myself so much. I love people who are real with me. Their friendship is invaluable. Anyway, up until that point I never thought of my mindset as a self-loathing person? I just thought that I honestly didn't measure up in certain areas. It was then that I realized that I was hating myself. Not only, did I have self-hatred, I was essentially saying what God made was substandard, when he said what he made was wonderful (Psalms 139:14).

How about you? How do you see yourself? Do you see yourself as less than anyone or anything else? If asked the question right now, "Do you love yourself?" Could you answer in the affirmative about every aspect of your being?

Survival Tip #6 - Reflection Questions

1. Define the word love.
2. What physical feature do you love most about yourself? Why?
3. What is your favorite personality trait? Why?
4. If given as a percentage, how much of you do you love? Explain.

∞ ∞ ∞

Real Life Application – Journal Entry #6

Do this for yourself. You may want to make sure no one will interrupt you during this exercise. Go to a place that has a full-length mirror and where you can close the door and have privacy. I'll wait. Ok, are you ready?

I want you to strip down to your birthday suit and stand in front of your full-length mirror. I want you to carefully look at yourself starting at your toes and slowly working your way up. When you get to the top of your head, start the process all over again. This time start at your feet and instead of filling your head with all the things you don't like about yourself, I want you to say at least three things you appreciate about each body part. Again, you will do this starting at your feet and working your way up to the top of your head. This time, take note of your facial expression as you say these things OUT LOUD to your yourself. You will do this for a third time, but this time you will say to yourself, *I am beautifully and wonderfully made by God for a purpose. I am one of a kind never to be duplicated. I am loved.* You will say this as you look over every inch of your body. By saying this out loud, your soul hears it. Repeat this exercise at least two to three times a week until you begin to believe this in your heart and soul.

There is something intimate about bearing your heart to others. There is something even more life-changing about bearing your heart, body and soul to yourself. So often we never take the time to truly look at, appreciate, and love how unique and beautiful we are. Applaud yourself for taking the first step of loving and valuing yourself. When you love and value you, how you treat yourself changes. When your relationship with yourself changes, your relationships with others begin to change, too. Now that we have worked on you, it's time to work on you working on him.

A Survivor's Guide

Survival Tip #6 Notes

WIFE TO BE

Survival Tip #6 Notes

A Survivor's Guide

Recipes for Chocolate

Peppermint Chocolate-Covered Strawberries

(V, GF, P) – *antioxidants*, vitamin A & C*

Ingredients:

- ¾ cup vegan and GF sweet, semi-sweet, white or dark* chocolate nibs or chips (I prefer dark chocolate. It increases endorphins, which boosts mood.)
- 15 semi-frozen strawberries
- Parchment paper
- 2-5 drops peppermint extractor 1 drop of peppermint oil (optional)

Directions:

1. Wash strawberries. (I spray them with a small amount of apple cider vinegar, then quickly wash them).
2. Put them on a paper tower to dry. It is important that the strawberries do not retain water as it will water down the chocolate, making it difficult to get the chocolate to stick later on.
3. Prepare chocolate dip as instructed below.
4. Dip the strawberries into the chocolate and place on parchment paper.
5. Refrigerate for about an hour and enjoy.

Chocolate Dip:

1. Add the chocolate nibs/chips to a double boiler. Stir frequently.
2. Add 1-2 drops of peppermint extract to liquified chocolate (optional). Once chocolate is liquid, dip is ready.

WIFE TO BE

Almond Chocolate Muffins (GF, P)

– Antioxidants, protein, vitamin E, iron

Ingredients:

- 1 ½ cups fine almond flour
- ½ cup finely chopped almonds
- ½ cup chocolate chips
- ⅓ cup maple syrup
- 2 eggs
- 2-3 tbsp avocado or olive oil (depending on your oven)
- ¼ cup cranberries or orange peel (optional)
- 2 tbsp flaxseed meal (optional)
- ¼ tsp baking powder
- ½ tsp salt
- Paper muffin cups and tins

Directions:

1. Turn oven on to 375°F.
2. Mix all wet ingredients together let sit for 2-5 minutes.
3. Mix all dry ingredients together.
4. Mix wet ingredients into dry ingredients with a mixer or by hand.
5. Line muffin pans with paper muffin cups.
6. Pour mixture into muffin cups.
7. Bake on 350°F for 25 minutes or until muffins are tested and cooked thoroughly inside.

Survival Tip #7

I Think I May Need a Drink:
A Man's Deepest Need

About four or five years into marriage, my nagging nature reared its ugly head again. I remember nagging my husband about something I had asked him to do days, perhaps weeks, before. It probably was the third time I had mentioned it. Omar turned to me with anger and disappointment in his eyes and said, "Sometimes, I like to think it is *my* idea instead of you always nagging me, telling me what to do. I'll do it when I'm ready."

Wow! I come from a stock of strong, independent women. We take nothing off of any man. Yet this statement stopped me in my tracks. It taught me a few things. First, his response allowed me to see that my husband had feelings. Believe it or not, up until this point I didn't think he cared about anything other than football. (This was mainly due to my upbringing, but that topic would fill a whole other book.) Second, it opened my eyes to the fact that I was acting like his mother and not his wife. A wife is supposed to be on equal playing field with her husband, not lord over him or be his personal conscience. In our family, we call this being someone's Personal Holy Spirit (PHS).

Since that day, I began asking Omar only once for whatever it was I needed. If it wasn't done (I had to give him grace, he wasn't going to change overnight), I took it to the Lord in prayer. I was floored at how much actually was achieved through simple, earnest prayers. God did more with one prayer than I could have done with a whole year's worth of nagging.

If love is not a man's deepest need, then what is? My friend, this is where you may want to get a drink and sit down because the real meat and potatoes of this book is about to be served. I know you may be thinking it is a three-letter word that starts with S and ends with X. But men have a deeper need that's far beyond sex. As Aretha Franklin said (I'm probably dating myself here), "R-E-S-P-E-C-T! Find out what it means to me!"

For men, being respected is much more important than being loved. I am not saying that men don't want to be loved. But if they had the choice, they would most likely choose to be respected over being loved. There is just something about that machismo.

Every man is different in the way he receives and perceives respect. This is where knowing your man comes into play. Ask yourself, what are his likes? What are his dislikes? Does he feel good when you compliment him in front of others or does that make him feel uncomfortable? If you decide to clean the house, does he notice and does his attitude improve? Simple little things that we, as women, may never in a million years think of can impact our husbands. If you are unsure of how to make him feel respected, ask him. Don't feel like you have to know it all. Rome wasn't built in a day. Relationships take time.

All men are different, but here are some general ways that men feel respected by their wives.

Give him eye contact when you two speak, especially when he is sharing the events of his work day.

Nearly all men feel most respected when they are heard. We as wives have this incredible opportunity to make our men feel like the king of the castle just by listening to the words they speak and responding, or not responding, accordingly.

I learned this one day when I was reading messages on my phone while my husband was talking to me. I wasn't particularly listening. Omar paused. He cleared his throat. I didn't notice. He cleared his throat again and asked if I was even listening to him. I tried to assure him that I was. When he asked me what he'd just said, I was a little lost for words. Omar repeated that he was talking about how people at work don't listen to him. BAM! Here I was, his wife, too preoccupied to do the very thing that he was feeling dejected about in the first place. All I did was just pour salt into the poor man's wound.

Let's go back to Survival Tip #2, when we talked about creating that place of safety and refuge in our marriage. I admit I was failing miserably in that department that day. I'm so sure he wasn't feeling very safe with or respected by me at that moment. I looked into his eyes and saw a defeated man. My friend, let me tell you, there is nothing more disheartening and hard to live with than a man who feels defeated. So, take advantage of this simple opportunity to build him up.

When he does something you are proud of, even if it is miniscule, let him know.

I know you are thinking, I am his wife, not his momma. But just try it and see how far your praise goes. I guarantee it will go a great deal farther than any verbal battering or criticism ever will. In fact, you may find he is finally doing the things you asked him to do with joy. Praise is a powerful tool.

It is so easy to see the faults. At times, they almost seem to dare us to utter them aloud. Be strong. We must realize that we gather more bees with honey than with vinegar. Besides, if the shoe were on the other foot, wouldn't you rather hear praise instead of pestering? Treat him like the person you want to be married to and he will rise to the occasion.

Praise the things that he does well and pray about the rest!

When we see things that are just not right, it is tempting for us to try to be our husbands' Personal Holy Spirit. But I assure you, no matter how much wives nag, we cannot create this metamorphosis within our husbands. In the immortal words of the Wise Woman, "You didn't create him, therefore you can't change him, no matter how hard you try." That statement stuck with me. She was so right. I could nag until I was blue in the face and the only result was deep-seated resentment and frustration for us both.

Relationships are a learning process. It takes time to learn how he ticks. Kudos to you for reading this book and creating a learning curve for yourself. You now have discovered why microwave marriages do not last. I am not saying I have all of the answers, because I do not. I do however, have a quarter century of trial and error and trial and win experiences.

Survival Tip #7 - Reflection Questions

1. How do you speak to your spouse? Do you honor him with your words? List some things you typically say to him.

2. If someone spoke to you the way you speak to him, would you be pleased or offended? Why?

3. How can you honor your spouse and show him respect? Write them down. Do them. Don't delay!

4. How do you like to be honored and shown respect?

∞ ∞ ∞

Real Life Application - Journal Entry #7

Ask your husband to describe things you can do to make him feel honored and respected. Make sure neither of you is stressed when you ask him this question. Write down what he says. Take one task per week, or one task per day if you're feeling adventurous, and do it.

A Survivor's Guide

Survival Tip #7 Notes

WIFE TO BE

Survival Tip #7 Notes

A Survivor's Guide

Smoothie Recipes

Smoothing things out in marriage takes effort.

Luckily these smoothie recipes do not.

CGE Island Mixer (serves 2) (V, GF, P)

- Vitamin C & K, protein, fiber

Ingredients:

- 3 mini cucumbers
- ½ tsp lemon juice
- 1 cup milk (almond milk tastes pretty good)
- 1 cup frozen mangoes
- ½ cup pineapples
- 1 stalk celery chopped
- 2 tbsp flaxseed meal
- Mint to garnish (optional)

Directions:

1. Blend cucumbers, celery and milk
2. Add mangoes, pineapples then blend
3. Add lemon juice and flaxseed meal, blend until smooth
4. Garnish with mint and chia seeds and serve

Eat Your Greens Smoothie (Serves 2) (V, GF, P)

- *Vitamin A & K, iron, folate*

Ingredients:

- 1 medium cucumber (do not peel)
- 1 bananas
- 1 handful spinach
- 1 green apple
- 2 cups water or nut milk
- 2 tbsp flaxseed meal
- Chia seeds to garnish (optional)

Directions:

1. Blend spinach, cucumbers and water/milk
2. Add in bananas, apple and flaxseed meal, blend until smooth
3. Garnish with chia seeds or greens and serve

Survival Tip #8

A Supplemental Pill Just Won't Do

"Do not let your adornment be merely outward—arranging the hair, wearing gold, or putting on fine apparel— but let it be the hidden person of the heart, with the imperishable quality of a gentle and quiet spirit, which is precious in the sight of God." - 1 Peter 3:4, NKJV

Early in our marriage, when Omar and I argued intensely, I believed that my way was the right way. No matter what the argument was about, I always believed my way was correct. In most cases it generally was, but that is beside the point. During one particular argument, we were in disagreement about a friend. Without revealing too much, I will say that one of us had a friendship that could be perceived as out of alignment. In other words, one of us believed that this friendship was not helping the new direction we were heading in, and the other believed it was a healthy friendship that had no negative bearings on that direction. Omar believed he was correct in his belief and, yet I knew *I* was in the right in my belief. I would not let up until my husband saw things my way, too.

I could hear my wise mentor loud and clear. "Remember the gentle and quiet spirit that 1 Peter talked about." I was feeling anything but gentle and quiet. Normally, I would argue until Omar either gave up or walked out. This time, however, I decided to give this gentle and quiet spirit thing a try. Not only was I quiet, but in the midst of my silence, I was praying. Now, at first, they were selfish prayers. They sounded a bit like this: "Lord, make him see that he is wrong and I am right. Make him apologize, so that I can try to forgive him."

Oh man, as I write this I can see I was really a piece of work. Then the prayers changed to "Lord, help him see my side of this situation so we can work this out." Not long after the prayers sounded like this: "Lord, please help me see things how You see things. If I am wrong, let me know it beyond a shadow of a doubt and help me to quickly seek to make things right so we can move on and be one again."

WIFE TO BE

My mentor, the Wise Woman, who declared that I did not create my husband, therefore, I cannot change my husband, also shared this scripture with me.

"In the same way, you wives, be submissive to your own husbands so that even if any of them are disobedient to the word, they may be won without a word by the behavior of their wives, as they observe your chaste and respectful behavior. "Do not let your adornment be merely outward—arranging the hair, wearing gold, or putting on fine apparel— but let it be the hidden person of the heart, with the imperishable quality of a gentle and quiet spirit, which is precious in the sight of God." - (1 Peter 3:1-4 NASB)

Gentle and quiet spirit? I was cool and hanging in there until she said *submission* and *quiet*. Coming from a single-parent background that birthed women of intense will and self-sufficiency, that S-word made my blood boil. Every fiber in me said, "I will be submissive to no man."

It wasn't until I fully unwrapped that word and unearthed its full meaning and potential that this scripture came alive in my house. I refer to our dwelling place at this particular time as a house because it wasn't until this submission revelation that our house began to be a home. Did I lie down like a doormat and let my husband run and rule all over me? No, I did not. Anyone who knows me knows in the immortal words of Sweet Brown, "Ain't nobody got time for that."

Although I thought submission meant catering to my husband's every whim, it was quite the opposite. The King James Version dictionary defines submit as "to yield without murmuring" (https://bit.ly/2GK6Nbb). There we go with that nagging subject again. According to Google it means to "agree to refer a matter to a third party for decision or adjudication" (https://bit.ly/2GtJZwv). In Ephesians 5:22 this word is used again. It talks about wives submitting to their husbands as unto the Lord. Here is where it really gets good. Submission in this context refers to you only doing that which falls in line with the One who created you; no more, no less. Finally, Google and I agree. There is a first for everything right? When I am submitting to my husband I am not submitting to him, I am referring the matter to a third party, God, for Him to render His decision or adjudication. I have now taken the pressure of the fight out of my hands and placed it in God's hands. Now I'm not saying that in being submissive to my husband, I'll kowtow and do all that he wishes. For example, if my husband were to ask me to do something that went against God's law, like invite other people into our marriage bed, or break the laws of the land (that do not go against God's word), that would be a no-go. God speaks against such things. However, it does mean that my husband may ask me to be more attentive to him, to cook, or — God forbid — to clean! In those cases, I would have to do things that are contrary to what I may normally want to do. Submission, however, is not just one-sided. In Ephesians 5:21 both husband and wife are commanded to show respect, or be submissive to, one another. In this example, God is showing us the importance of communicating and yielding to the needs of the other. It is a partnership.

1 Peter 3:1-4 became and still remains my anthem scripture. I have lived with submission, and I have lived without. I will take living with submission any day of the week. When a yielding of the wills regularly occurs in the marriage, you will have a marriage that is built on mutual respect and reverence for each other, not a war of wills.

Survival Tip #8 - Reflection Questions

1. How would you define submission?

2. How would your spouse define it?

3. Do you believe that doing something your husband asks without complaining would make a difference in how you two communicate in the future? Why or why not?

∞ ∞ ∞

Real Life Application - Journal Entry #8

Building upon the Survival Tip #7, Create three columns on a piece of paper. Title the first column "Things (your spouse's name) asked me to do." Write down 5 things your husband has asked of you that you may have responded to with a bit of attitude. Title the second column "My reaction." Here you will write your reaction to each request. Title the third column "A better choice." Here you will write how you could have responded to your husband's requests more pleasantly.

There may be many things we don't want to do in marriage. Our response to our husbands' requests, however, can either turn a molehill into a mountain or a mountain into a molehill.

A Survivor's Guide

Survival Tip #8 Notes

Survival Tip #8 Notes

A Survivor's Guide

Recipes that Speak to Your Man's Heart

Raspberry Honey Wings (GF, P)

- Protein, vitamin C, manganese

Ingredients:

Main Dish

- 2 lbs. chicken party wings
- 1/3 cup apple cider vinegar
- ⅓ cup raspberries
- 2-3 tbsp raw honey
- ¼ tsp sea salt
- ¼ tsp turmeric
- ¼ tsp black pepper
- ½ tsp garlic

Dipping Sauce

- ¼ cup Dijon mustard
- ¼ cup mayo (I love avocado mayo from Costco)

Directions:

Raspberry vinegar

1. Blend apple cider vinegar with honey and raspberries in a food processor
2. For extra zing add 1 tsp orange peel (optional)

Main Dish
3. Wash and season wings.
4. Put wings in pan and drizzle raspberry vinegar over wings.
5. Bake on 400 for 25-30 minutes or until completely done.
6. Mix mustard and mayo together let sit for 5 minutes. Serve.

WIFE TO BE

Quick Spinach, Garlic & Dill Cassava Wraps (V, GF, P)

– Vitamin C, manganese, potassium, folate

Note: This is a gluten and grain-free version. I use them for personal pizzas, tacos, wraps, pinwheels and more.

Ingredients: (Serves 6)

- 1 cup cassava flour (Otto's brand works best - Amazon)
- 2 tbsp olive oil plus 1 tsp for cooking
- ¼ tsp garlic powder
- ¼ tsp dried dill
- ¼ tsp sea salt
- 2 handfuls of spinach
- ½ cup of water

Directions:

1. Mix spinach and water in a blender until it is an even liquid consistency.
2. Add flour, salt, garlic and dill in a bowl and mix well.
3. Add oil and spinach mix to the flour to make a dough. ***Add spinach, mix slowly. *** All of it may not be needed. Use just enough to make achieve a dough-like consistency.
4. Roll into 6 balls (golf-ball size).
5. Place dough ball between two pieces of parchment paper. Flatten with a tortilla press or by hand with a roller.
6. Heat olive oil in a pan over medium to low heat. Make sure the pan is hot before adding tortilla. Cook until there are brown spots on each side (roughly 45 seconds on first side and 30 seconds once flipped).
7. Place between parchment paper until ready to serve.

A Survivor's Guide

Survival Tip #9

Eat Your Veggies to Be Strong

I think you have come to know that we are a military family. At one point, both my husband and I were U.S. Army soldiers. When I was six months pregnant with my daughter, I was finally stationed together with my husband in Ft. Bragg, NC. We had been married for two years. We had previously been stationed separately around the country and would visit each other during breaks. One summer break, when I was traveling from San Antonio to D.C. by way of North Carolina, was particularly good. I guess you can conclude that is how I got to be six months pregnant. For about a year before my arrival, my husband lived in a mobile home about a mile or two outside of Ft. Bragg. He lived there with two other single soldiers. Upon my arrival, we had a difficult time trying to find housing that would accommodate a family. We finally settled on a duplex that was maybe a total of seven hundred square feet if we were lucky. It smelled like a sewer and the rent equaled almost an entire paycheck, but I was able to tolerate that because it had a washer and dryer in the unit. That is so valuable and missed when you live exclusively in the barracks. The best bonus, however, was that I finally got to be with Omar. We were technically still newlyweds since this would be the first time we would be living together since our wedding day. I was so excited.

A few days after we settled in, he brought me to his workplace to meet his coworkers and friends. As I waddled through the office, everyone stared at me. I couldn't blame them. I know my belly was a little on the big side. I am five feet tall on a good day and I was *all* belly. The surprised looks my husband's friends gave when they saw me in all of my round belly splendor were unmistakable. Neither one of us had married friends. Our lives never really warranted them. We were considered geographical bachelors by the Army. This is the term used when you are married but your spouse is stationed elsewhere. As geographical bachelors, we lived in barracks or with other single soldiers. Just short of forming strong bonds with the opposite sex, our lives mirrored that of a single person. We were at the cusp of tasting that lifestyle's bitter fruit.

I envisioned marital bliss. He would be home with me at night and we would snuggle as couples do. He, on the other hand, saw business as usual. He and his single friends would go out, while I remained at home. Needless to say, it caused quite a rift within our marriage. Looking back, we both see the naivete of our actions and thought processes. We wanted a blissful, married life without giving up the lifestyle we had grown accustomed to while living apart. Our marriage started deteriorating fast. It would not stop until we made a conscious effort to change who we kept as company.

Remember when your mother told you that in order to be strong you must eat your veggies? I remember a cartoon I used to watch when I was child. This character used to eat these green leafy veggies all the time. He said it made him strong and after downing a can of them he could fight off even the toughest of opponents. Well that may be a little far-fetched, but there is strength to be gained from veggie fuel. Vegetables do give you nourishment to be strong. Just as vegetables do that for our physical bodies, our friends do this for our marriages. The advantage of friends is that we get to do life together with them. The disadvantage of friends is that we sometimes do life with them when we shouldn't. I have learned over the years that your friends should have a life status similar to yours. It took us quite some time to get the hint that our friends were dividing us and not helping us to grow together. One of his single friends had been divorced already because of a very similar scenario.

I know I may get some flak for this one, but I stand by it because I lived it. Now please hear my heart on this. I am not saying that you or your husband should never have single friends. What I am saying is that those you hold close and dear should be ones that can walk through life with you, understand your struggles, encourage you and not wreak havoc on achieving a healthy environment in your home.

Sometimes there is a falling away of friendships because our lives change. Although it hurts, it is a part of life. Some people are with us for a lifetime, some for just a season, and others for only a particular reason. Understand that I am not saying desert all of your friends and spend time exclusively with your husband because that gets tired and old really quick. What I am saying is that you and your husband need to guard your union at all costs. Your marriage is your first priority. You've spent countless hours cultivating a relationship and pouring your heart into this person. Wouldn't you want to protect that investment as best as you could? In order to keep your marriage intact, one must be attentive to cultivating it at all times.

I bet you didn't bank on marriage coming with all of this work, huh? Well, the successful ones do. Trust me, it will yield you an extremely high dividend if you invest wisely. Just as eating a healthy diet will prosper and protect your physical body, having healthy friendships and cultivating your marriage will prosper your marital union.

Survival Tip #9 - Reflection Questions

1. Who are your friends?

2. Do you and your friends have similar lifestyles, goals, and visions for the future?

3. Do your friends support the bond you have with your husband or do they continue to invite and encourage you to do things that single people have liberty to do?

4. Do you feel conflicted between your relationship with your husband and your friendships with your girlfriends? If so, explain why.

5. Moreover, do you have guy friends who may be negatively impacting your relationship with your husband? *If so, how do you think your husband feels about these friendships?

6. *Perhaps your husband may feel insecure when you are with them. If your husband is truly the person with whom you seek to spend the rest of your life, you may need to take inventory of your outside relationships and evaluate what those associations are worth.

Real Life Application - Journal Entry #9

It is said that a person is the average sum of the five closest people to him or her. This statement means that one's life parallels or mirrors the five closest relationships to them. Evaluate the five friendships that are the dearest to you. Ask yourself if you would be content with your life mirroring what you see in theirs, not in a comparative sense, but in the way of walking in the same direction as they are walking. If the answer to this question is no, perhaps this is a friendship that may need to be reevaluated in light of your present dreams and goals for you and your husband.

A Survivor's Guide

Survival Tip #9 Notes

WIFE TO BE

Survival Tip #9 Notes

Veggie Recipes to Keep You Strong and Him Happy

Veggie Pita Filling (V, GF, P)

- *Omega 3 & 6, B vitamins, vitamins C & D*

Ingredients:

- 1-bushel kale chopped
- 4 portabella mushrooms sliced
- 4 artichoke hearts (in a glass jar in water)
- 5 sweet peppers sliced
- 1 small onion diced
- 1 clove garlic chopped
- 3 dates chopped
- Dipping sauce from chapter 8
- ½ cup water

Directions:

1. Sauté all ingredients in a skillet (in water if not using a nonstick pan)
2. Serve over pita wrap (see chapter 8)

Twist and Shout Cleangoodeats Collards Greens (V, GF, P)

– *Vitamin A, B6, E & K*

Ingredients:

- 1-bushel collard greens chopped
- 1-bushel kale chopped
- ½ cup carrot shreds
- ½ cup cranberries
- ¼ cup cottage cheese (I prefer the block cheese)
- ½ small onion
- 1 clove garlic
- 1 tsp coconut oil
- 1 ½ tsp apple cider vinegar

Optional sauce:
- 2 tbsp avocado mayo (I love Costco's bran
- 1 tbsp balsamic vinegar

Directions:

1. Sauté coconut oil and onions in a skillet.
2. Add kale and collards (stems removed).
3. Add rest of ingredients and sauté.
4. Mix ingredients or sauce together in a bowl and then add sauce (optional) to pan stir until fully mixed in (about 30 seconds), turn off heat and serve.

Survival Tip #10

Old-School Home Cooking:
Find a Mentor and a Mentee

I still treasure almost 20 years later the valuable words of the "Wise Woman" I've mentioned in almost every chapter of this book. Her words were, and still are, precious nuggets of gold. She was my mentor for a time. In fact, we only knew each other for a few months, but it's amazing how impactful one's life can be on another. As you recall me telling you, some relationships are for a lifetime, some just for a season and others for a reason. I had a deep need in my life for her for a season and a reason. Without her, I honestly believe I would have never known how faithful God could be, especially in times of distress, or how amazing a marriage can be when we are willing to be teachable. Her words coupled with the life she lived turned light bulbs on in my head. The whole experience demonstrated that I don't have to make all of the mistakes myself, and neither do you. God will provide people along your path to guide you to walk upright and not stumble all over yourself. Bumps and bruises are a part of life and having someone to patch you up and carry you until you are well again is priceless.

Other women have come into my life and shared wisdom that I have carried with me along life's journey. My mother who showed me how important it is to value and respect myself, and that people will treat you the way you allow them to treat you. Then there was my nana. She showed me the importance of being and behaving like a lady. She also stressed the importance of fixing home-cooked meals. She would tell me the secret ingredient in EVERY meal she made was love.

I remember having a conversation with her one morning as she was preparing breakfast. She said I would need to learn how to cook one day. At that time, I had this amazing superpower of invisibility when it was time for meals to be made, then miraculously reappearing to devour the finished meal in its entirety. But on this day, I couldn't escape. Nana was onto my game and closed off all avenues for my jailbreak.

I answered her, "I won't need to know how to cook when I grow up because everything will already be made for me and all I will have to do is heat it up."

She laughed at me almost like a mad scientist. Then she flared her nostrils in the way only Nana could do. She looked me sternly in the face and said, "Your husband will need to eat."

I laughed on the inside because I dared not laugh on the outside and get my head knocked off. But I said, "Nana I am not getting married. So, no worries there."

She glared at me and chuckled, "We'll see."

When Omar and I were dating, I got the bright idea to cook for him. I wanted to impress him by making barbecue chicken. Never mind that I didn't know how to cook. I placed the oven on 450° F and cooked the chicken for about 15 minutes. I soon figured out I was running short on time and thought upping the temperature would cook the food faster. When we sat down to eat, Omar cut the blackened chicken open and blood oozed all over his plate. There was an awkward silence. He looked at me, smiled, and said, "Want to go out to eat?"

Although that moment is funny now, it was almost earth shattering when I remembered my Nana's bold wisdom and prophecy. "Your husband will want to eat." I began thinking, well, if Omar doesn't come back, then I guess he wasn't marriage material in the first place. Imagine my joy when he did return even after I had almost killed him with that meal!

It wasn't until then that I embraced how valuable Nana's lessons really were. It turns out that she was correct. I *did* need to learn how to cook. God blessed me with a man who cannot eat any packaged goods. Nothing that has any preservatives, dyes or soy products can grace his plate because of a condition Omar has. So there went my theory of having already prepped foods available. God has a funny way of getting his point across. Somehow, I think He and Nana had a conversation. I just can't prove it.

Any successful marriage first starts with two successful people. I don't mean people who are rich, scholarly or have it all together. Success just means that you are a person who is pliable, receptive and willing to continually grow. Successful people know that they have not arrived. Successful people know that relationships take work. No marriage became victorious overnight, nor did it happen in a bubble. Any flourishing marriage you see had people behind the scenes helping it look flawless. A movie production has key actors in the film, but there is a whole crew behind the camera that brings it together. There is the director, assistant director, screenwriters, understudies, key grip (I still have no clue what a key grip does), etc. A marriage is no different. No, you don't get to have a stunt double, although I prayed for one on several occasions. You do get to have a screenwriter, director, supporting actor, and understudy. These are the people to help you along the road you are traveling, so that when you find those landmines called disagreements, you have both seasoned and unseasoned couples who will get you both across the minefield with as few casualties as possible.

The Oscar-Winning Movie, I Mean Marriage Crew

The Director - This is your mentoring couple. They are the seasoned pair who willingly shares their experiences, both good and not so good, so you do not have to relive them all within your marriage.

The Supporting Actor - Also known as the side-by-side couple who lives on the same level playing field as your marriage. Perhaps you both have kids who are close in age, or you both are close in age, or have been married for about the same number of years. This couple is invaluable. The two of you can join with other couples within this level and enjoy the fellowship of each other's company. They can take your children at a moment's notice when you need a break or just want to have alone time with hubby. Of course, this is also reciprocated, so choose wisely and carefully. If they have bad behind kids, you do not need that level of stress in your life! Trust me!!!

The Understudy - These are your mentees. Perhaps they are yet to be married, just at the beginning stages of engagement, or serious about wanting to spend the rest of their lives together. They may be newly married and still have the love glaze over their eyes. Understudies help to keep your skills in marriage sharp. It's just like with children. They are always watching. They use us as guides. When we teach or advise others we sharpen our own skills. It makes us more cognizant of how we treat our spouse, especially when we know there are other sets of eyes watching us.

Survival Tip #10 – Reflection Questions

1. We talked about a mentoring couple. What do good directors (mentors) look like to you? What attributes should they possess?

2. What do you feel are three key characteristics that a supporting actor (side-by-side couple) should have?

3. What can you provide to an understudy (mentee)?

∞ ∞ ∞

Real-Life Application – Journal Entry #10

Finding a mentor, side-by-side couple and mentee is not always an easy task, but it is a necessary one. Looking back on your relationship assessments from Survival Tip #9, are there any people who fit the description you gave in the answers to this chapter's Reflection section? If not, don't fret. These types of relationships take time.

Make a list with three columns. Title these columns "Mentor," "Side-by-side," and "Mentee." Using your lists from this chapter's reflection section, write down names of people you think embody those characteristics. Now you have a starting point. You may need to revise this list time and time again, but it is a great start to get you thinking. Once you have narrowed down your list to at least one person per column (can be more than one, you are not limited), let your relationships with these people form organically. That means there is no need to be formal unless you feel the need to be. These types of relationships are best nurtured in natural, casual ways.

A Survivor's Guide

Survival Tip #10 Notes

WIFE TO BE

Survival Tip #10 Notes

A Survivor's Guide

Old School Home Cooking

These are recipes my nana would make. Well, she swore up and down that if I gave away her secret macaroni and cheese recipe she would come back from the grave and get me. So, the following recipes are my take on some of my nana's best dishes.

Baked Macaroni and Cheese (GF, P)

– Calcium, vitamin D, potassium, protein

Ingredients:

- 2 blocks seriously sharp cheddar cheese (The cheese makes the difference. Only seriously sharp cheese will do. To avoid artificial colors, use white cheese.)
- 1 box elbow macaroni (I use lentil or chickpea elbows to keep it GF, but feel free to use whatever you wish.)
- Almond or Coconut milk (dairy milk may be used as well) enough to coat the bottom of the pan to maintain moisture
- ½ tsp sea salt
- ½ tsp paprika
- ½ tsp pepper
- ¾ tsp garlic
- 1 egg

Directions:

1. Boil macaroni until done (I use veggie broth in lieu of water to add more flavor)
2. Preheat oven to 400° F
3. Shred cheese
4. Mix cooked macaroni, cheese and seasonings
5. Add egg and mix everything together. Make sure the macaroni has cooled down a bit to prevent scrambling and cooking the egg
6. Layer macaroni and cheese in a 9x13 pan
7. Place a layer of cheese on the top with extra pepper and paprika
8. Pour milk over macaroni, this will lightly coat the bottom of the pan. Cover the pan and cook for 25 minutes.
9. Take cover off and cook until macaroni begins to crisp on the top.

Fried Turkey Sliders (GF, P) – *protein, fiber, choline*

Ingredients:

- 1 cup brown rice flour (store-bought or home ground)
- 2 tbsp chia seeds
- 8 slices thick turkey breast (already cooked)
- 1 egg
- Avocado or coconut oil (use only if not using a nonstick pan)
- 1 tsp smoked paprika
- ½ tsp pepper
- ¼ tsp sea salt
- 1 tsp garlic
- 1 tsp curry
- Any other seasonings you enjoy

Directions:

1. In a bowl, mix flour, chia seeds and seasonings
2. Scramble egg in separate bowl.
3. Preheat pan (with oil if not using a nonstick pan).
4. Dip turkey slice in egg. Coat with flour mixture and place in pan when oil is sizzling.
5. Cover pan and cook on each side until brown.
6. Drain oil by placing in a colander with a paper towel under it.

A Survivor's Guide

Survival Tip #11

Develop the Neck Bone:
The Man is the Head but the Woman is the Neck

Growing up, the power of manipulation was modeled well. I saw how easy it was for a man to be swayed into agreement on just about any topic. I must admit to you, on many occasions, I did use this to my advantage. But there is one thing about manipulation that I didn't always see, and this is it comes back on you with a vengeance. Married life has taught me a few things. The first lesson is there is a proper order that needs to be established so that the marriage will function like a well-oiled machine. Men were made to be the head of the household. That is the order of God's design. Just as with any organization or establishment there is an order of hierarchy. Marriage was designed for God to be at the helm, the man to follow God and for the woman to follow the man. In reading this you can easily deduce that the woman is to be subservient to her man, following him all over the place. I would ask you to refer back to chapter #8, A Supplemental Pill Just Won't Do, to understand that this is simply not the case.

It is true that God made the man the head of the household, which means he is ultimately responsible for what goes on within the home. Which, if you think about it, as a wife this takes a huge load of weight off of your shoulders. We will address this in my next book "Intimacy Begins in the Kitchen".

God did put the head on the neck, as you know. The head weighs approximately 8% of the body's weight. It takes strength and flexibility to hold the head and support its weight. The neck connects the head with all of the other vital organs of the body. Without the neck the brain could not function to tell the heart to beat, or the liver to filter or the lungs to breathe. These all belong to vital systems within the body, yet none could operate or co-exist without the neck fulfilling its purpose and without its proper placement beneath the head. Is the neck any less important than the head? I would say emphatically no. When there is any trauma to the neck via airflow or blood flow the brain is directly impacted and suffers. Therefore, the role of the neck is not subservient to the head, the fact that the neck is located below the head is merely placement. The head directs, the neck assists. The head responds, the neck supports. In addition, the neck provides balance and flexibility. Tension headaches occur when the muscles in the head and neck begin to contract, this causes pain to occur behind the eyes, making it painful to see. A tension headache also causes pain around the forehead, making it difficult to think clearly, and sometimes severe pain in the neck making it difficult for the neck to be flexible and do its job adequately. There are many conditions that can lead to a tension headache. Cold temperatures, food and specific activities may be a culprit, as well as diseases such as the cold or flu. Another lesser talked about irritant is stress. Stress can cause muscle contractions in both the head and the neck, bringing on moderate to severe pain in both the head and the neck regions.

You are probably thinking I started reading this book to learn how to be a better wife, not to get an anatomy lesson. This may be true, but it is in the anatomy where the truth of God's design of marriage is revealed. So, let's break this down. The head weighs approximately 8% of the entire body. In my opinion, I think the head weighs as much as it does because it houses the command center of the body. The head is intricately designed to withstand pressure and outside influence that the neck is not equipped to handle. The neck is an amazing mastery of balance, symbiosis and support, this is true. However, only when both are in optimal health will they yield fantastic results and the body will feel like it is in harmony. But throw a monkey wrench in the plan, like stress and the body's harmony is out of whack. Would you think it ridiculous for the neck to do the function of the head? Or how about the ear do the function of the eye? So why do we think it is ok for a wife to do the what God has instructed the man to do? Now if the man is not living up to what God has called him to do, then that is a completely different scenario. But if that is not your story, you need to help your household be in correct alignment again.

This is not a natural behavior for women. If you are anything like me, you are a take charge kind of woman. When something is not getting done, you step in and make it happen. To understand the origin of this behavior we must look to the book of Genesis, in chapter three Adam and Eve sinned in the garden. Before God threw them out of the Garden of Eden, He tells Eve that she will want to rule over her husband. First this is the basis of why God commands us to respect our husbands, but also it gives us the origin of why we often feel the need to execute our husbands' role within the marriage. Often times manipulation plays a part. When we usurp that authority, the peace and harmony that God planned for marriage is also usurped. We must remember that our role as the neck is very important. We have the pleasure of being able to influence our husbands to make good choices. Since we have this role, we also have a high responsibility to not abuse it.

Survival Tip #11 - Reflection Questions

1. Use a dictionary to define "manipulation".
2. What do you think is the role of a husband in marriage?
3. What is the role of a wife in marriage?
4. Are you in agreement with those role descriptions? Why or why not?

Real Life Application - Journal Entry #11

Read Genesis 2:7-3:24. Journal a comparison to marriage the way God ordained it and then when humans decided to do marriage their way. Pay special attention to how they interacted with each other and with God.

A Survivor's Guide

Survival Tip #11 Notes

WIFE TO BE

Survival Tip #11 Notes

Thyroid Friendly Recipes

These Recipes help the thyroid which is a gland in the neck that regulates the hormones that control many facets of the body. Many people suffer with over and under active thyroids. This gland also controls mood. Something that we women no nothing about (said very sarcastically)

Fried Bananas (V, GF, P) – *Potassium, fiber, protein, iron*

This recipe has a crunchy, sweet taste it is the perfect treat for your sweet tooth and texture cravings.

Ingredients: (serves 2)

- 3 frozen medium bananas thickly sliced
- ½ cup shredded coconut
- Coconut oil (enough to fry the bananas)
- ½ cup Maple syrup
- ½ cup nut-based flour (I used almond)

Directions:

1. Add coconut oil to pan with medium heat
2. Mix shredded coconut and almond flour
3. Dip banana slices in maple syrup, roll them in the coconut flour mixture
4. Fry until brown
5. Add sweetener of choice to bottom of cup pour golden milk on top, stir
6. Serve

Salmon or Chicken Salad (GF, P)

– *Omega 3's*, fiber, protein, iron, antioxidants*

Ingredients:

- 3 BPA-free cans of chicken breast or salmon*
- 3 Tbsp avocado mayo (Costco)
- 2 tsp balsamic vinegar
- 2 sweet peppers
- 2 stalks celery
- Handful of cranberries
- ½ large onion
- ½ tsp sea salt
- ½ tsp pepper
- ½ tsp smoked paprika
- ½ tsp garlic
- If you prefer your salad to be creamier add more mayo

Directions:

1. Mix all ingredients in a large bowl
2. Serve. Pairs nicely with the wrap in chapter 8, or over toast

WIFE TO BE

A Survivor's Guide

Survival Tip #12

Aphrodisiacs-R-Us: The Sex Factor

I Don't like preplanned robotic exercise. There, I said it. I don't. To me it is boring. I like spontaneity. Make it a playful game and I will exercise all day. Volleyball, football, obstacle course your name it. I view premeditated, planned sex the same way. This is the sex you have when children have taken over your life, landmines called Legos are strewn all over your floor like daggers to one's feet, and you value sleep above all else in life to include but not limited to oxygen. If you haven't had the pleasure of pre-planning under this type of duress, just wait, it really is like entering the twilight zone.

I recall a few times having to psyche myself up for it. I would have a routine that went something like this.

- Get up...check (yes it was just that serious sometimes)

- Take a shower...check

- Turn on "mood" music...check

- Pack a sultry romantic note written by me, the love of his life (had to remind myself of this, especially when I looked like who done it and ran), for him to find in his lunch bag...check

- Spray perfume on paper so anticipation mounts as he smells it all day...check.

Perhaps midway through the day a text would come with just a wink or catchy phrase that only the two of us would understand. We never knew when other eyes would be prying while we read each other's text messages. When I arrived home, I would quickly get dinner on the table and get the little rug rats, I mean children in the bed. I would jump into the shower again, to be able to focus on him. Focus is so important. Women can think of a million things all at one time. Men, on the other hand, in the same situation have only one thing on their brains and it won't depart until it is accomplished. I never understood that, yet I am thankful. It assured me that with this wonderful endearing quality, he is thinking of me and not pondering if he finished the laundry or failed to pay a bill. Do you see why that second shower for us women is so important? Once we both actually make it into the bed, the goal is not to fall asleep before reaching the mountaintop. If we both accomplish this oh the wordless conversation that takes place. This is where the magic happens. Yes, *Lord* this is where we get to the good stuff. When God said the two shall become one. He spoke some of the loveliest words EVER! This is where communication on its deepest level occurs. The in-depth conversation can (and should) only happen with your spouse. You don't (or at least you shouldn't) have this closeness with anyone else. To be able to communicate with another individual this intensely is a gift that should be cherished. Often times we view it as a battle of the sexes. "I will do it to get it over with so he will leave me alone." Or "I will do this *for him* so he will do that *for me*." But the physical act of sex has wonderful emotional and spiritual implications.

Now this scenario may seem a bit far-fetched to you, but when you are married in the beginning love making is spontaneous, like little bunnies wherever you go. When a man gets use to that it is bliss to him. However, understand just because the dynamic changes, his need, yes, I said need, for sex does not change. Sure, you have been dealing with two toddlers under the age of three. Throw up is your un-chosen perfume for the day and your hair is disheveled when your husband walks through the door with "that" smile on his face. Please know that the second shower or perhaps even a bath is necessary. When your marriage hits this phase both of you will need to make adjustments, but do not, I repeat, do not abandon this vital element of your marriage. It is hard to break up a marriage that is consistently consummated. When both partners look after and tend to the needs of the other, marriage undeniably works.

So back to my opener of not liking to exercise... After being with children all day, I didn't have the time, strength or brainpower to get to a gym. All I wanted to do was collapse in the bed. But I looked at making love to my husband as a playful act of exercise. I exercised physically for sure, but I also exercised my will to be in alignment with his. In doing this we connected in ways words could never describe, on a level that goes deeper than any other relationship.

Sex, the act of making passionate love to your spouse, is an intense form of communication. Your husband was designed to have his most intimate conversations in this manner. Be present for the dialogue. He will share so much with you. Make sure you are well focused on him to reciprocate the exchange.

Survival Tip #12 - Reflection Questions

1. What is your sex life like presently? Is it one of intimate conversation or "wham bam thank you ma'am"?

2. What aspects of it are pleasing to you? To your spouse? What would you change?

3. Do you make time for this vital part of your marriage? Why or why not?

∞ ∞ ∞

Real Life Application - Journal Entry #12

As you reflect on this most intimate part of your marriage have an honest talk with yourself. Ask the tough questions. Is sex a tool used for giving pleasure to your spouse, or just receiving pleasure? Is a tool used for manipulation? Are you both satisfied with the level and frequency? If not, what do you think should change? Journal and talk with your spouse about this.

A Survivor's Guide

Survival Tip #12 Notes

WIFE TO BE

Survival Tip #12 Notes

A Survivor's Guide

Aphrodisiacs – Foods to Fuel Your Fire

Sweet Potato Hash (V, GF, P) – *fiber, vitamin C & A,*

Ingredients:

- 2 large Sweet potatoes diced into medium sized chunks (do not peel)
- 4 Yukon gold or small red potatoes diced
- ¾ cup cranberries
- 1 Vidalia onion (spiralized or diced)
- 1 clove garlic (diced)
- ½ tsp smoked paprika
- ¼ tsp (plus a pinch) of salt
- ¼ tsp black pepper
- 1/2 tsp turmeric
- 1 TBSP coconut oil
- Water to coat the whole bottom of the pan
- Maple syrup optional to taste

Directions:

1. Turn skillet on to medium heat.
2. Place a very thin layer of coconut oil in the pan
3. Add onions and garlic and sauté
4. Once onions begin to brown just a bit (caramelize) add the rest of the veggies (not the cranberries) and the seasonings
5. Add water enough to coat bottom of pan and a little more
6. Mix veggies with onions and garlic then cover for about 5-7 min. until sweet potatoes begin to soften make sure the water does not dry out. Add more if you need to.
7. Uncover and add cranberries mix until all potatoes are softened, but not mushy.

My Little Fruity Drink (V, GF, P)

– Antioxidant, vitamin A, K & C, folate, calcium

Ingredients: (serves 2)

- 1 cup frozen strawberries
- 1 cup frozen watermelon
- ¼ cup arugula
- 1 cup kombucha (unflavored) or ginger ale or seltzer

Directions:

1. Blend arugula and kombucha well
2. Add watermelon and strawberries blend well
3. Serve with mint as a garnish

WIFE TO BE

About the Author

Sakinah Bunch, is the witty, CEO of Cleangoodeats. She is also a wellness ambassador, health coach, Army veteran, Army spouse for more than two decades and mother of three.

While working as a professional style consultant, Sakinah discovered her daughter was allergic to all but four foods, then her husband was diagnosed with an incurable, food-related chromosome disorder, she had to learn to cook – fast. Her struggles inspired her to delve fully into researching the effects of food on the body and on the family. She relinquished her day job to pursue this new passion full time. This led her to create Cleangoodeats, which reconnects families by teaching healthful cooking and holistic wellness. Sakinah is an international educator who shows people how to make allergy-friendly, gluten-free and specialized meals, taking the stress out of mealtime and bringing the family back to the table.

She learned over the years that balancing work, maintaining a happy, healthy marriage and raising a family with allergies was not an easy feat. Through her trials and triumphs, she has made it her mission to share her knowledge with others. As she says, she "manages to keep them alive with style, love, humor and plenty of Cleangoodeats!"

Sakinah speaks all over the world on topics related to marriage, connecting families together through healthy eating choices, cooking, and allergy related topics. For bulk orders and to book Sakinah for speaking events, call 502-233-3020 or email cleangoodeats@gmail.com.

Want to be a part of our WIFE TO BE community and receive more recipes, encouragement from Sakinah and WIFE TO BE community members, be the first to know about live events and conferences with Sakinah and more? Connect with us on Cleangoodeats.com.

Index of Recipes

Almond Chocolate Muffins, 60

Apple Crisp with Vanilla Banana Ice Cream, 49

Baked Macaroni and Cheese, 98

Banana Mango Ice Cream, 13

BBQ Cauliflower Bites, 37

CGE Island Mixer, 68

Chicken or Mushroom Stew, 22

Coconut-Crusted Flounder, 39

Eat Your Greens, 70

Fried Bananas, 109

Fried Turkey Sliders, 100

My Little Fruity Drink, 120

Mushroom, Spinach, and Coconut Soup, 20

Peppermint Chocolate-Covered Strawberries, 58

Pulled Jackfruit, 11

Quick Spinach, Garlic and Dill Cassava Wraps, 80

Raspberry Honey Wings, 78

Red, White and Cream Coconut Delight, 51

Salmon or Chicken Salad, 110

Sweet Potato Hash, 118

Twist and Shout Cleangoodeats Collard Greens, 90

Veggie Pita Filling, 88

A Survivor's Guide

www.ingramcontent.com/pod-product-compliance
Lightning Source LLC
Chambersburg PA
CBHW040457240426
43665CB00038B/13